volume
2

NAOKI URASAWA

HUFF

HUFF

HUFF

PROFES-
SOR!

Chapter 9 ◉ That Thing

HUH?

MR NAKAIDO, WHAT IS A SCHOLAR'S GREATEST ENEMY?

IT ISN'T?

...OR BUREAU-CRATS CUTTING RESEARCH FUNDING.

IT ISN'T HARD-HEADED ACADEMICS...

...WHO ABANDON THEIR OWN RESEARCH!

IT'S THE SCHOLARS...

THAT MAN'S BEHAVIOR...

...IS SUSPICIOUS!

IT'S JUST, THE INFORMATION IS COMING FROM SUCH AN UNRELIABLE SOURCE.

TH-THIS ISN'T ABOUT GIVING UP.

EVERY MOUNTAIN WE MAKE IT OVER, HE ASKS FOR MORE MONEY.

INTERPRETING IS MY JOB.

N-NO! DON'T INTERPRET THAT!

HE'S FLEECING US FOR A FORTUNE!

HE'S RIGHT, MR. NAKAIDO.

AND THIS IS *OUR* JOB—OUR MISSION!

!!

OH, HOW PROFES- SIONAL OF YOU.

TEN METERS BEYOND THIS POINT...

...WE MAY MAKE A REVOLUTIONARY DISCOVERY.

UGH...

WE'VE COME TOO FAR TO TURN BACK NOW.

WOULD YOU HAVE DOUBTED GALILEO?

CONSIDER *HISTORY*, MR. NAKAIDO!

!!

8

AW, NOT AGAIN...

PSST WHISPER WHISPER WHISPER

HA... HA... HA...

PLEASE, WAIT.

HOW MUCH?

I KNEW IT.

HE DOESN'T WANT TO GO ANY FARTHER, SO...

FIVE DOLLARS?! TEN?!

WE'RE CLOSE! HOW MUCH DO YOU WANT?!

PROFESSOR?!

THREE HUNDRED DOLLARS.

THREE HUNDRED DOLLARS.

N-NO!

PRO-FESSOR!

OKAY, OKAY.

...

AGREED! NOW LEAD ON!

AT 360 YEN TO THE DOLLAR...

HUH? TH-THREE HUNDRED?

SAY NO, PROFESSOR!

...TH-THAT'S 100,000 YEN!

HUH?

DON'T DO THIS, PROFESSOR! THEY'RE—

ARRRGH! IT'S NO USE!

10

PRO-FESSOR YODO-GAWA!!

WHERE DID YOU GO?!

P-PRO-FESSOR?!

DON'T LEAVE ME BEHIND!

P-PRO-FESSOR...

OH...

PRO-FESSOR!!

TUMP TUMP

WHOA...

TUMP

WHAT IS THAT?

HUH?

NOW YOU SEE. THIS IS WHY WE CAME ALL THIS WAY!

W...

OH M-MY...

THESE ARE *THAT THING'S*...

...CLAW MARKS!

C-CLAW MARKS?

TO LEAVE BEHIND CLAW MARKS LIKE THESE...

...THE CREATURE WOULD HAVE TO BE *COLOSSAL*!!

THAT'S IMPOS- SIBLE.

NO WAY...

14

BUT CLAW MARKS THIS BIG...

...SUGGEST IT'S MUCH LARGER THAN EVEN A BLUE WHALE!

THE SIZE IS ALL WRONG.

YOU ESTIMATED IT'D BE THE SIZE OF A KILLER WHALE.

IF WE'RE DEALING WITH THE SAME SPECIMEN...

THAT'S RIGHT, NAKAIDO!

THE WITNESS SIGHTINGS WERE FROM ONE YEAR AGO. IT APPEARS THE SITUATION HAS CHANGED.

...!!

...IT'S GROWING AT A FRIGHTFUL PACE!

WHEN DID THESE MARKS APPEAR?

A YEAR AGO, BUT HE'S TOO FRIGHTENED TO SAY MORE.

HE'S ABSOLUTELY TERRIFIED.

...

BUT THEN IT'D BE EVEN BIGGER NOW! HA HA HA!

ULP...

HAVE YOU ACTUALLY *SEEN* IT?!

DOES THAT MEAN...

HM?

WELL, HAVE YOU?!

ASA...

ASA?

ASA!!

MY HOUSE!

THAT FOOTPRINT IS WHERE MY HOUSE WAS!

IS THAT REALLY WHERE IT WAS?

I'LL FLY OVER AGAIN!

Y-YES!

CALM DOWN! NO FOOTPRINT IS THAT BIG!

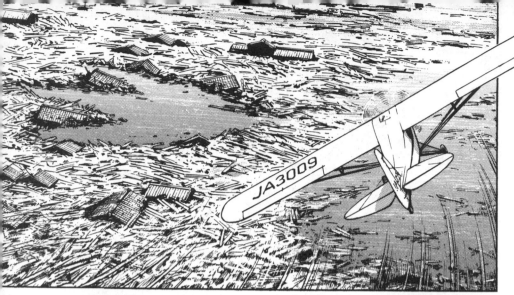

IS THAT OKURA'S HOUSE?!

OVER THERE!!

WHAT ABOUT *YOUR* HOUSE?

AND THAT'S...

...TAKEDA'S HOUSE.

AND?

PSHTT

FLY OVER TO THE LEFT.

PSHTT

*BALLOON: YOSHIMARU DEPARTMENT STORE

I SAW SOME PEOPLE ON A ROOFTOP.

HM?

COME ON, TELL ME.

OH?

DROP!

TELL ME WHEN TO DROP.

WE HAVE TWO BAGS OF RICE BALLS.

GET READY...

R-RIGHT.

ONLY ONE BAG LEFT.

WE SHOULD GO BACK FOR MORE.

BECAUSE I LOVE YOU. ♪

?

...ASA ASADA...

HEY...

ASA!!

MISTER, DO YOU SEE ANYONE ON THE RIGHT?

BECAUSE I LOVE YOUUU. ♪

BECAUSE I LOVE YOU. ♪

...

I DON'T KNOW THE NAME OF THAT SONG, SO I CAN'T REQUEST IT ON THE RADIO.

MISTER, I PROMISED YOU.

HUH?

WHAT ABOUT *YOUR* HOUSE...?

...

I PROMISED I'D NEVER CRY AGAIN.

...BUT I'M NOT GOING TO CRY!

MY HOUSE IS GONE...

AND I WON'T GIVE UP!!

...AND GIVE IT TO MORE PEOPLE.

FOR NOW, WE'LL GO BACK FOR MORE RICE...

...

...YOU'RE RIGHT.

Y-YEAH...

THOSE CHILDREN ARE SIGNALING FOR HELP. THERE'S EVEN A BABY.

LOOK OVER THERE.

WE SHOULDN'T WASTE TIME.

AND THE O.B.! DOCTOR TANAKA!!

SHINROKU!! HAZUKI!!

HURRY!

GO BACK!

IS THAT YOUR FAMILY?

AND THE DOCTOR'S HOLDING THE BABY!

THEY'RE MY LITTLE BROTHER AND SISTER!

OVER THERE! HURRY BACK!

DON'T LOSE SIGHT OF THEM!

?!

EASY, NOW. AN AIRPLANE CAN'T JUST SPIN AROUND. BUT I KNOW WHERE THEY ARE!

WHAT'S THAT?!

HURRY, HURRY!

WHAT *IS* THAT?!

HUH?

28

THEY HAVEN'T NOTICED IT!

!!

RUUUN!!

RUN, EVERY-BODY!!

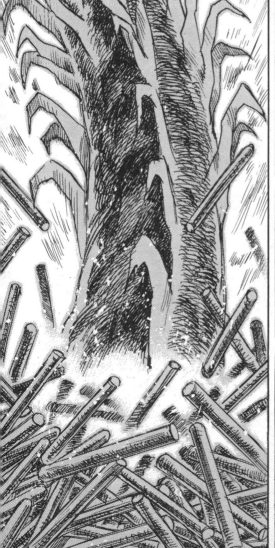

IT'S COMING UP BEHIND YOU!!

THEY'RE TOO BUSY WATCHING THE PLANE!!

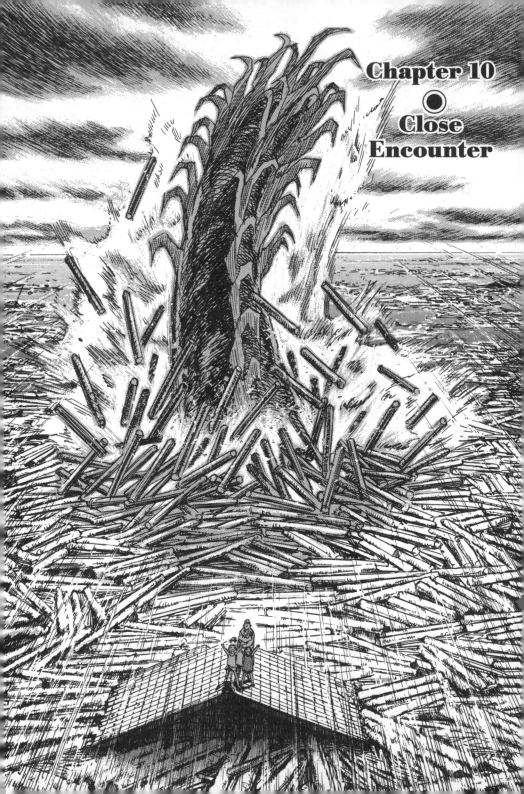

Chapter 10
●
**Close
Encounter**

...YOU GREEDY PIGS!

RUN FOR THE RICE BALLS...

DROP!

UWAH!

SHINROKU! HAZUKI! DOCTOR TANAKA!!

IT D-DISAP-PEARED!!

LET'S HOPE THEY'RE ALL RIGHT!

ARGH!

SHIN-ROKU! HAZUKI! DOCTOR TANAKA!!

BUT IT COULD COME BACK ANY MINUTE!

TO THE RIGHT! AT THREE O'CLOCK!!

WHERE ARE THEY NOW?

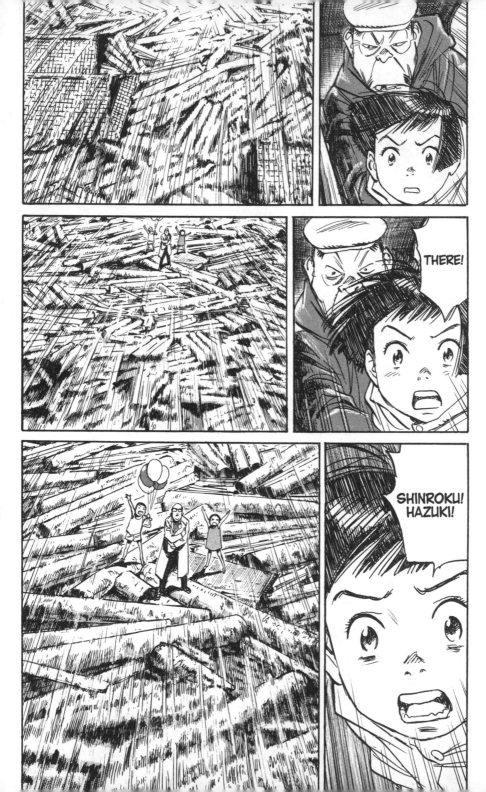

WE'LL BE BACK SOON!

IT SOUNDED LIKE ASA...

WAS SOMEONE SHOUT-ING?

HM?

THAT BABY'S A NEWBORN!

LET'S FOCUS ON GETTING MORE RICE BALLS FOR NOW.

BUT WHERE IS SHE?

THAT MEANS MOM GAVE BIRTH!

...PEOPLE SEE STRANGE THINGS.

WELL, IN EXTREME SITUATIONS...

HEY, MISTER?

WHAT WAS THAT THING?

RIGHT.

AND POW-DERED MILK!

YOU THINK WE WERE HALLUCI-NATING?!

HUH?

40

BUT THAT THING REALLY *WAS* BIG AND SCARY!

FEAR ONLY MAKES THE ENEMY LOOK BIGGER AND SCARIER.

I SAW HORRIFIC SIGHTS DURING THE WAR.

ANYWAY, DON'T GIVE IN TO FEAR.

DON'T TELL ANYONE ELSE ABOUT THIS. THEY'LL ONLY IMAGINE THE WORST.

HUH?!

YES, MA'AM!

GRAB SOME POW- DERED MILK!

YAHOO!

THE BABY WAS ALL RIGHT?!

I'M SO GLAD!

THE POLICE HAVE BEEN WORKING NONSTOP SINCE LAST NIGHT! AND NEED I REMIND YOU THERE'S NO LANDING AIRPLANES ON PUBLIC ROADS?!

WHERE'S THE RESCUE TEAM?

HEY, OFFICER.

YEAH?

THE SELF-DEFENSE FORCES? THEY'RE SPREAD THIN.

THIS MESS IS UP TO THE POLICE!

WHAT ABOUT THAT NEW FORCE THEY PUT TOGETHER?

THE POLICE CAN'T HANDLE THIS.

FOR A RESCUE EFFORT?! WHY?!

HEAVY WEAPONRY?!

GUESS WE'D NEED THE GOVERNOR TO MOBILIZE THE SDF...

THE SDF'S PROBABLY TOO GREEN TO STAND A CHANCE ANYWAY.

YOU WOULDN'T BELIEVE ME.

WELL, TELL YOUR SUPERIORS YOU NEED HEAVY WEAPONRY.

ARE YOU ALL RIGHT? YOU LOOK PALE.

HM?

HEY.

...

43

...

FIX US UP A NICE MEAL LATER, YEAH?

I'M JUST HUNGRY.

HERE! WE'VE GOT THE MILK!

YES?

HEY, OFFICER.

NOW GET GOING!

THANK YOU!

I CAN'T BELIEVE THIS!

HUH?! ME?!

SPIN THE PROPELLER.

SO HURRY UP. A BABY'S WAITIN' FOR MILK!

I CAN'T PARK HERE, RIGHT?

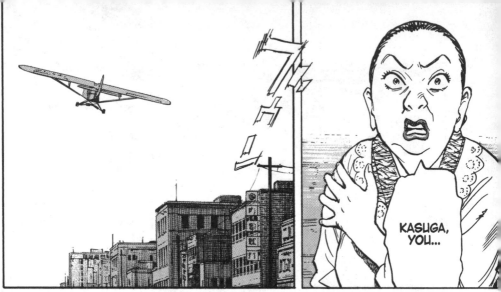

KASUGA, YOU...

EVERYONE'S SO NICE!

NOW I JUST NEED TO BLOW UP MORE BALLOONS.

THEY EVEN MADE THE MILK FOR ME!

I'M SO GRATEFUL FOR THEIR HELP.

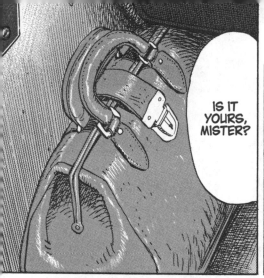

IS IT YOURS, MISTER?

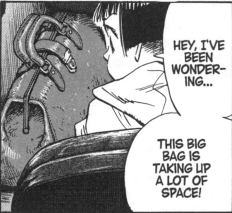

HEY, I'VE BEEN WONDERING...

THIS BIG BAG IS TAKING UP A LOT OF SPACE!

PCHAK

WHAT'S INSIDE?

CAN I LOOK?

WHAT IS THIS?

HM?

YOU'RE SO NICE, MISTER!

YOU HAD POWDERED MILK FOR THE BABY ALL ALONG!

OH! MORE POWDERED MILK!

IT AIN'T MILK.

THAT WHITE POWDER...

OH, I GET IT.

POW- DERED MILK?

...THAT SLIMEBALL SHOT AT ME.

GUESS THAT'S WHY...

W- WHAT'S WRONG?

MISTER ?

SOME-BODY SHOT AT YOU?

YOU'RE BLEEDING ALL OVER! WHAT HAPPENED?!

HUH?

...BUT IT'S WORSE THAN I THOUGHT.

I WISH I COULD TELL YOU NOT TO WORRY...

I CAN'T FEEL ANYTHING WITH MY RIGHT HAND.

BUT LIKE I SAID...

...I'M A HERO OF THE SKIES.

BECAUSE I BIT YOU? NO, THAT WAS YOUR LEFT...

LOOK. WE'RE GETTING CLOSE.

WHEN I'M AT THE CONTROLS, I CAN SAVE ANYONE.

HUH?!

...AND USE EXTRA BAL-LOONS.

PACK THE BOTTLES WITH THE RICE BALLS FOR PADDING...

OKAY, I'M ON IT...

SHINROKU! HAZUKI! DOCTOR TANAKA!

...DROP!!

ALL SET!

...AND...

READY...

WAIT THERE! HELP WILL COME SOON!!

OKAY! THEY GOT THE MILK!

YOU DID GOOD, MISTER!

...

MISTER!

MIS-TER?

UNGH...

MISTER!!

D-DID THE BABY... GET THE MILK?

COME ON, MISTER! HANG IN THERE!

UH... YEAH.

NOW IT WON'T GO HUNGRY!

YES! THANKS TO YOU!

...THAT'S GOOD...

OH...

MISTERRRR!!

ASADORA!

ASADORA!

NOW HOLD STEADY!

DISTANCE TO ENEMY, 1500! ALTITUDE, TEN! BANK RIGHT TEN DEGREES!

WELL?!

AND NOW THINGS GET HAIRY!

THE CHANCES ARE THE SAME AS A LIGHTNING STRIKE!

ARRRGH!!

NOTHING HAPPENED!

WHOA...

ULP...

DESTROYER, STRAIGHT AHEAD!

Chapter 11 ○ At the Controls

MIS-TER...

I...

I...

MISTER...

MISTER!!

MISTER! TELL ME WHAT TO DO!

...ANY-THING.

I CAN'T FEEL...

WHAT'S WRONG, MISTER?!

OW!!

URGH... I'LL USE MY LEFT...!

YEAH, IT'S BLEED-ING TOO.

MY LEFT'S NO GOOD EI-THER!

OKAY, GOT IT!

KTAK

EYES AHEAD! STRAP IN!

IS THAT BECAUSE ...

...I BIT YOU?

GRAB THAT STICK IN FRONT OF YOU!

WE'RE REALLY CLOSE TO THE WATER!

WAH!

...

AND TILT IT IN THE OPPOSITE DIRECTION!!

HUH?

...TILT IT THE OTHER WAY!

WE'RE LEANING ONE WAY, SO...

...UNTIL...

PULL SLOWLY...

NOW SLOWLY PULL IT TOWARD YOU UNTIL YOU CAN'T SEE THE GROUND.

...THE GROUND.

...I CAN'T SEE...

GLANCE TO THE SIDE TO KEEP US LEVEL!

BUT NOT TOO MUCH OR WE'LL CLIMB!

...THE GROUND...

LEVEL WITH...

JA 3009

MISTER, I—

I'M REALLY DOING IT!

MISTER!

I'M FLYING!

MISTER!!

MM?

I GOTTA SAY...

...I FEEL SORRY FOR YOU, KID.

WHAT DO I DO NOW?!

WHAT NOW?

I DID NOT! BESIDES, WE'VE GOT OTHER PROBLEMS!!

...AND THAT MAKES LIFE HARD.

YOU LOST FAMILY...

HUH?

YOU MUST RELY ON KINUYO...

SHE'S A TOKYO WOMAN WHO OPENED A SHOP IN NAGOYA.

THAT SIGN WAS A LANDMARK FOR SOLDIERS COMING BACK FROM THE WAR...

*SIGN: DINER KINUYO

RATTLE

BACK THEN, A WOMAN'S NAME ON THE SIGN OF A DINER ACTED AS A BEACON...

...YOJIRO KOMATSU?

DID YOU KNOW...

ARE YOU KINUYO?

I WAS WITH HIM IN SIBERIA.

...TO COME AND TELL YOU...

AND HE WANTED ME...

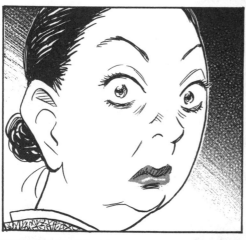

...IF HE EVER DIED.

SHE CAN HELP YOU.

RELY ON KINUYO.

RIGHT NOW, YOU'RE ALL I'VE GOT!

NOT RIGHT NOW, SHE CAN'T!

JUST YOU! THE HERO OF THE SKIES!!

...OF THE SKIES...

HERO...

WHAT'VE I BEEN DOING...?

Y-YEAH...

THAT'S RIGHT! YOU'RE UNBEATABLE AT THE CONTROLS, RIGHT?!

OF COURSE I CAN...

BUT YOU CAN MANAGE, RIGHT?!

...RIGHT NOW...

BUT...

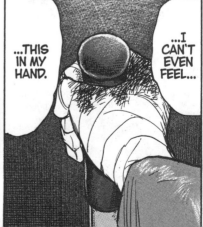
...THIS IN MY HAND.

...I CAN'T EVEN FEEL...

TMP

TMP

TMP

小牧総合運動場

*SIGN: KOMAKI GENERAL ATHLETICS FIELD

TMP...
TMP...

TMP

TMP

HM?

76

CLOMP CLOMP

WHAT'S WRONG, SHOTA?!

NO ONE SAID YOU COULD STOP!

BUT YOU SAID...

...A TIDAL WAVE SWEPT AWAY OUR HOUSE.

...I'M WORRIED ABOUT ASA...

I DON'T FEEL LIKE RUNNING ANYMORE.

AW, DON'T FRET OVER THAT!

HUH?

...BUT...

I'M GLAD WE'RE ALL SAFE...

FORGET THEM. JUST FOCUS ON MAKING THE OLYMPICS!

ASADA? OH, THAT HUGE FAMILY?

ASA? WHO'S THAT?

FROM THE ASADA FAMILY.

THERE'S AN ASA TOO. SHE'S REALLY FAST.

DO THEY EVEN HAVE A DAUGHTER NAMED ASA?

I DON'T KNOW. I THINK THERE'S A YAYOI OR SATSUKI, BUT...

W-WELL, UM...

SHE'S FAST? DID SHE BEAT YOU IN A RACE?!

WHAT'D YOU JUST SAY?

W-WELL, UH...

SHE DID?!

SAVE ROMANCE FOR AFTER THE TOKYO OLYMPICS!

UH... WHAT?

WHAT'S WRONG WITH YOU?

SH-SHE'S ONLY IN SIXTH GRADE!

R-ROMANCE?

WHAT A WEAKLING! LOSING TO AN ELEMENTARY SCHOOL GIRL!

START RUNNING, LOSER!

AND SHE BEAT YOU?!

HUFF

HUFF

HUFF

YOU CAN WORRY ABOUT GIRLS LATER!

GIVE US TEN MORE LAPS!

ASA...

HUFF

HUFF

HUFF

HEY...

ASA...

WHERE ARE YOU GOING?!

STOP, SHOTA!

ASA!!

ASADORA!

ASADORA!

INJURED?!

KASUGA.

WHO IS?

...HIS RIGHT SHOULDER IS BLEEDING!

YES. I DIDN'T NOTICE BEFORE BECAUSE OF THE COLOR OF HIS RAINCOAT, BUT...

THAT OLD PILOT?

I DOUBT IT BELONGS TO HIM...

WHERE'D HE GET THAT AIRPLANE ANYWAY?

THEN WHAT'S HE DOING FLYING AN AIRPLANE?

HEY...

HUH?

THAT'S THE LAST THING WE NEED TO WORRY ABOUT RIGHT NOW!

I SMELL A CRIME!

...HE MIGHT LOSE CONSCIOUSNESS!

IF HE'S FLYING IN THAT STATE...

WHAT WILL HAPPEN TO ASA?!

WHAT WILL HAPPEN TO THE GIRL WITH HIM?!

ULP... UH...

ARE YOU JUST GOING TO ABANDON HER?!

SHE LOST HER HOME TO THE STORM, BUT SHE'S STILL OUT THERE DELIVERING FOOD TO OTHER SURVIVORS!

H-HOLD ON A SEC-OND!

N-NO, UH...

...NEED TO HELP HER!

YEAH! THE POLICE AND THE SDF...

AFTER ALL, THEY'RE WAY UP IN THE CLOUDS...

HUNH?!

WHAT CAN I DO?!

...I COULD USE MY LEFT HAND!

URGH! IF ONLY...

?

...THE OPPOSITE OF THE DIRECTION WE'RE LEANING...

THEN PULL IT BACK...

...

...A LITTLE SO WE DON'T CLIMB...

MISTER, NOW THAT THIS BAG'S UNDER ME...

...AND GLANCE TO THE SIDE TO KEEP US LEVEL.

THIS IS PRETTY EASY!

...I CAN SEE MUCH BETTER THAN BEFORE.

OH, UH...

ARE YOU SAYING PILOTING IS EASY?

WHAT'S SO FUNNY?

HEH HEH...

...YOU'RE DOING GREAT.

NO...

...SOUND SO COCKY.

SORRY, I DIDN'T MEAN TO...

I'M NOT SURE HOW...

...TO DESCRIBE THIS FEELING.

THAT MEANS A LOT COMING FROM YOU!

REALLY ?!

*RAINCOAT: TANAKA OBSTETRICS

IT'S MY FIRST TIME FLYING A PLANE, BUT...

...I FEEL LIKE I'VE BEEN DOING IT FOREVER!

...

IS THAT A WEIRD THING TO SAY?

CUT THE NON-SENSE AND KEEP PRAC-TICING.

MY PRAISE WENT TO YOUR HEAD.

YES. IT IS.

YOU'RE NOT A REAL PILOT UNTIL YOU *LAND.*

WELL, AIRPLANES DON'T STAY UP FOREVER.

PRAC-TICING?

...TOWARD THOSE SMOKE-STACKS ON THE LEFT.

SWING US AROUND...

USUALLY, YOU'D ALSO USE THE PEDAL, BUT FOR NOW FOCUS ON THE STICK.

HOW DO I DO *THAT?*

EYES FORWARD AND DON'T TILT TOO MUCH.

DUMMY! DON'T TILT TOO FAR!

OKAY!

IF YOU LET UP ON IT, WE'LL DESCEND.

DON'T LET THE NOSE DIP, DUMMY!

JUST BARELY PULL IT TOWARD YOU!

OKAY!

LIKE AN EGG...

OH, RIGHT!

GRIP IT GENTLY, LIKE AN EGG!

YES?

UM, OFFI-CER?

HOW ARE THINGS DOWN AT THE PORT?

THIS ISN'T LEISURELY...

NO, UH...

IT'S HARDER THAN IT LOOKS!

HUH?

THIS IS NO TIME FOR A LEISURELY JOG!

BEATS ME! UH, HEY!

94

R-RECOVERY EFFORT?! DO YOU MEAN THE PORT'S BEEN TOTALLY DESTROYED?!

NEVER MIND THAT! HEAD TO THE PORT AND HELP WITH THE RECOVERY EFFORT!

...

...GIRL?

ELE-MENTARY SCHOOL...

MEANWHILE, THAT ELEMENTARY SCHOOL GIRL IS SAVING LIVES!

AW, YOU'RE USE-LESS!

OFFICER! THERE YOU ARE!

AIR-PLANE?

SHE'S IN AN AIRPLANE DELIVERING RICE BALLS TO PEOPLE WHOSE HOUSES ARE UNDERWATER!

YEAH! YOU SHOULD BE MORE LIKE HER!!

HAVE YOU SPOTTED ASA'S AIRPLANE?

THEY SHOULD'VE RETURNED FROM DELIVERING THE MILK A LONG TIME AGO!

NO, NOT YET.

ASA?!

UM...

WHAT IF SOMETHING'S HAPPENED TO HER?!

N-NO NEED TO SHOUT AT ME, MA'AM!

!!

HERE THEY COME !!

IS SHE, UM...

THAT GIRL IN THE AIRPLANE...

HEY, UM...

HUH? REALLY?!

INCOMING AIRCRAFT!

WHAT'S HER FAMILY NAME?

YES!

...A BOB HAIR-CUT?!

THAT ASA GIRL! DOES SHE HAVE...

!!

ASA ASADA!

ASADA!

*SIGNS: (RIGHT) DAITOKU CO., (BACK LEFT) NITTO, (FRONT LEFT) YAKUMO

ASA...

...IS UP THERE?!

WHERE'RE THEY GOING?! THE RUNWAY STREET ISN'T THAT WAY!

THEN EASE FORWARD TO LOWER THE NOSE.

FIX YOUR EYES AHEAD AND A LITTLE DOWN.

THE FIRST RUN IS PRACTICE.

BUT DON'T LOSE SPEED.

AT THE SAME TIME, PULL THE THROTTLE ON THE LEFT.

STAY AT 50 MILES PER HOUR.

FEEL IT ALL...

FEEL YOUR ATTITUDE, SPEED, ALTITUDE AND DIRECTION ON INSTINCT.

DON'T FOCUS ON THE INSTRU- MENTS.

AS SHE SETS DOWN, LEVEL HER OUT...

...AND COM- PLETELY CLOSE THE THROTTLE.

...ON INSTINCT!

THROTTLE WIDE OPEN! STEP ON THE RIGHT RUDDER PEDAL SO YOU DON'T VEER LEFT!

YES! YOU DID IT! NOW UP!

...

WHY DIDN'T THEY LAND?

HM?

CAN YOU HANDLE THIS, ASA?

YOU BET I CAN, MISTER.

NOW FOR THE REAL LANDING.

...ALIVE!

I'M GONNA GET YOU ON THE GROUND...

I GOT THIS UNDER CONTROL.

NOW I'M HEARING IT FROM A KID.

THAT'S WHAT I ALWAYS TOLD MY CREW.

HA HA...

STRAIGHT DOWN...

...ONTO THE STREET!

...AND PUSH FORWARD TO LOWER THE NOSE!

LOOK AHEAD AND SLIGHTLY DOWN...

...AND STAY AT 50 MILES PER HOUR!

CLOSE THE THROTTLE...

...AND WHEN IT COMES TO ATTITUDE, SPEED, ALTITUDE AND DIRECTION...

DON'T FOCUS ON THE INSTRUMENTS...

...FOLLOW YOUR INSTINCTS!!

HERE I GO, MISTER!

COME ON!!

GOOD JOB, GIRL!

PAT PAT

YOU'RE AN IMPRESSIVE AIRCRAFT!

YOU HAD ME WORRIED, BUT YOU DID IT!

RIGHT, MISTER?

...WE CAN'T CELEBRATE EVERY BIRTHDAY.

SINCE MY FAMILY'S SO BIG...

...BUT WE DON'T DO THAT AT MY HOME.

I'VE HEARD ABOUT BIRTHDAY PRESENTS...

I EVEN SKIP MY *OWN* BIRTHDAY.

FAMILY IS WHAT'S IMPORT- TANT...

IT'S MORE IMPORTANT TO KEEP FOOD ON THE TABLE AND GET ALONG WITH EACH OTHER.

...IS ACTUALLY MY BIRTHDAY.

YOU KNOW, TODAY...

...BUT THIS ISN'T THE TIME...

...TO WORRY ABOUT THAT.

...I KNOW WHAT I WANT FOR A BIRTHDAY PRESENT.

AND FOR THE FIRST TIME...

ALL I WANT IS...

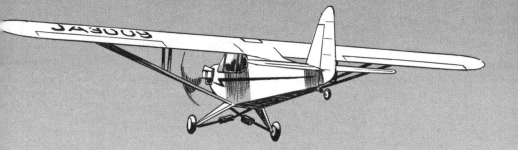

MY FAVORITE IS THE ONE ABOUT A DRAGON CHILD WHO GOES SEARCHING FOR HIS MOTHER.

THE SCHOOL LIBRARY HAS A BOOK OF FAIRY TALES.

AFTER HE FINDS HER, THEY SAVE THE VILLAGERS BY CULTIVATING THE LAND.

...FLIES THROUGH THE SKY.

THE MOTHER TAKES THE CHILD ON HER BACK AND...

ASA ASADA...

YES?

THAT'S EXACTLY HOW THIS FEELS.

ASA...

...DO YOU REALLY WANT THIS AIRPLANE?

ARE YOU ALL RIGHT?!

I-I WAS JOKING! KEEP QUIET! I'M TRYING TO LAND!

NO, LISTEN TO ME.

HUH?

JUST BE QUIET AND—

IF YOU WANT THIS AIRPLANE...

THEY'RE REALLY LANDING THIS TIME!

OH MY!

ASA CAN'T SERIOUSLY BE FLYING THAT THING!

NO, IT'S TRUE!

ASA...

INCREDIBLE! YOU DID IT, ASA!

SHE REALLY IS THE PILOT!

YOU TRULY ARE AN AMAZING GIRL!

UNDERSTOOD! BUT ALL THE AMBULANCES ARE TIED UP AT THE PORT!

AND SOMEONE RESCUE MY SIBLINGS! THEY'RE BY BLESSED BATH!

NEVER MIND ME! GET HIM AN AMBULANCE!

DON'T DIE ON ME!

THE TRUCK YOUR PLANE NEARLY HIT WILL TAKE YOU TO THE HOSPITAL!

HANG IN THERE, SIR!

I GOTTA USE THE LITTLE GIRLS' ROOM.

OH, GO RIGHT AHEAD.

KINUYO, YOU SHOULD GO WITH HIM.

ASA...

HUH?

UM... NOTHING!

?

WHAT ARE YOU CARRYING?

122

HEY, UH...

...

...YOU'RE EVERYONE'S HERO.

ASA...

I CAN'T LET YOU SHOW ME UP.

JUST YOU WAIT!

I'M GONNA RUN IN THE TOKYO OLYMPICS.

*SIGN: TEMPURA

I'LL SHOW YOU!

HUFF HUFF HUFF HUFF

*SIGN: DINER KINUYO

125

CAREFUL! WHADDAYA WANT?!

!!

HM?

WILL YOU GIVE ME A LIFT?!

OH, MAN! JUST LOOK AT THIS LINE!

小牧飛行場
関係者以外立入禁止

*SIGN: KOMAKI AIRFIELD, AUTHORIZED PERSONNEL ONLY

PRESENT YOUR ENTRY FORM!

YEAH, SURE.

I'LL HOP OUT HERE. THANKS!

*SIGN: AIRFIELD OFFICE

COME IN.

CREAK

空港事務所

NOK NOK

CAN I HELP YOU?

TMP

TMP

TMP

TMP

HM?

NOK NOK

WHO IS IT?

...?

...THEN GIVE ME YOUR AIRPLANE!!

IF YOU WANT WHAT'S IN THIS BAG...

ASADORA!

ASADORA!

*SIGN: NAGOYA GENERAL HOSPITAL NO. 1

WAAAH!

YOU'RE ALIVE!

ARE THERE ANY CLEAN DIAPERS HERE?

WHEN ARE YOU GONNA EXAMINE MY BROKEN BONE?!

SORRY. WAIT YOUR TURN!

MY WIFE IS IN LABOR!

OH MY...

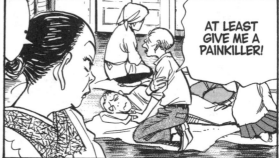

AT LEAST GIVE ME A PAINKILLER!

SIGH.

WAIT YOUR TURN!

UM—

OUTTA MY WAY!

IS THERE A MAN HERE WITH A GUNSHOT WOUND?

THE TRUCK CAME OUT OF NOWHERE AND THAT GIRL ZIPPED RIGHT OVER IT!

I'M TELLING YOU, IT WAS INCREDIBLE!

OFFICER!

WHOOSH! RIGHT OVER THE TRUCK!

I DON'T HAVE TIME FOR TALL TALES.

BUT IT'S TRUE, DOC!!

WHERE IS HE?!

...I GAVE HIM SOME AS A REWARD FOR HELPING PEOPLE OUT!

WHERE'S KASUGA?

OH...

THEY REMOVED THE BULLET, AND SINCE I HAPPENED TO BE HIS BLOOD TYPE...

DON'T WORRY.

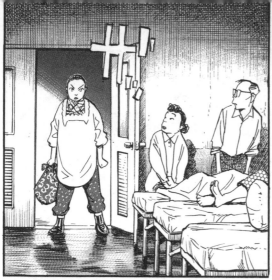

H-HEY! HE'S FINE NOW!

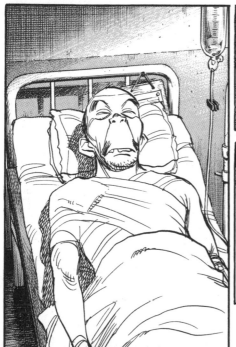

HEY...

KASUGA!

HOW COULD YOU?!

AND THEN THERE'S *THIS*!

THAT GIRL LEFT A NOTE BEHIND!

A LETTER AND A BUNDLE?

WHAT DID YOU SEND HER TO DO?!

OH NO...

WHAT "DEAL" IS SHE TALKING ABOUT?!

THAT DUMMY...

SHE'S ACTUALLY DOING IT.

A BIRTHDAY PRESENT.

WHAT BIRTHDAY PRESENT?!

WELL, SHE SAID SHE WANTED IT.

WANTED WHAT?!

TH-THEN WHAT ABOUT THIS?!

THE AIRPLANE.

Chapter 14 ● That Airplane

*SIGN: KOMAKI AIRFIELD, AUTHORIZED PERSONNEL ONLY

ARE YOU THREATENING ME?

THIS ISN'T A THREAT.

I JUST WANT TO TRADE THIS BAG FOR THE AIRPLANE.

WHICH IS BASICALLY A THREAT.

YOU'VE GOT BRASS, BRAT.

I'M NOT A BRAT.

A DEED OF TRANS- FER?

I GOT IT AT THE AIRFIELD OFFICE.

Name:

Deed of Transfer

Details:

The individual who has signed above here[transfers ownership of the aircraft specifi

Type or model of aircraft:

Aircraft manufacturer:

Aircraft number:

Aircraft registration:

Date of transfer:

NO, I CAME ON MY OWN!

I BET YOU'RE WORKING FOR THAT AIRPLANE THIEF.

YOU DID?

SO *YOU* WANT THE PLANE?

HOW YA FIGURE?

YES! IT'S BETTER FOR THE PLANE...

...IF I OWN IT INSTEAD OF YOU!

I'M A ROTTEN EGG, HUH?

A GREAT PLANE LIKE THAT SHOULDN'T GO TO WASTE ON A ROTTEN EGG LIKE YOU!

OF COURSE. YOU SHOT MR. KASUGA.

DON'T LET HIM FOOL YOU, MISS.

HE'S A *THIEF.*

BECAUSE HE TOOK WHAT'S MINE.

HE'S THE ROTTEN EGG.

BUT HE FLEW THAT PLANE TO DELIVER RICE TO VICTIMS OF THE TYPHOON ANYWAY!

YOU SHOT HIM AND NOW HE'S HURT!

HE ISN'T A THIEF OR A ROTTEN EGG!

HE'S A *TRUE HERO OF THE SKIES!*

AND HE HELPED ME LOOK FOR MY MISSING FAMILY!

IF HE DIES, I'M BLAMING *YOU*!!

...

...

YOU'RE STARTIN' TO BUG ME.

"THE GUY WHO SHOT MR. KASUGA IS AT THE AIRFIELD. I'M GOING TO MEET HIM AND MAKE A DEAL."

The guy who shot Mr. Kasuga at the airfield. I'm going to meet him and make a deal. The white powder is on a shelf in the shop.

"THE WHITE POWDER IS ON A SHELF IN THE SHOP."

HM?

THIS IS ALL DRUGS!

RATTLE KLATTER JOLT

OH DEAR...

WHAT'S THE HOLDUP? GET A MOVE ON!

I CAN'T. THERE'S A LINE.

THAT MAN HAS A GUN!

YOU CALLED FOR BACKUP, RIGHT?!

I LOST MY WALKIE-TALKIE IN THE CONFUSION FROM THE STORM!

HAVEN'T YOU NOTICED?!

I'M COMING WITH YOU!

WELL THEN, I'LL GO ON FOOT!

ENTRY FORMS!

ENTRY FORMS, PLEASE!

YOU **WHAT**?!

EVERYONE'S TOO BUSY TO COME ANYWAY!

ARGH! SERIOUSLY?!

SORRY, I CAN'T! LOOK AT THIS TRAFFIC!!

HEY, SECURITY! THERE'S AN EMERGENCY UP AHEAD. LEND ME A HAND!

FINE, WHAT-EVER!

YOU'VE GOT GUTS, GIRL.

YOU WANT TO MAKE A DEAL?

AND MAKE IT SNAPPY!

SHOW ME WHAT'S IN THE BAG.

PTAK

DO YOU KNOW WHAT'LL HAPPEN IF YOU HURT ME?!

!!

IT'S *EMPTY!* SO YOU TRIED TO PULL ONE OVER ON ME!

SO JUST FILL OUT THE FORM AND STAMP IT!

W-WHY YOU...

YOU'LL NEVER FIND OUT WHERE THAT POWDER IS!

...

THAT CRAZY KID...

ULP...

I CAN USE THIS BUNDLE AS A MAKESHIFT SHIELD...

I G-GOTTA STAY CALM...

NOT THAT IT'LL DO ANY GOOD.

KTIK

I JUST WANT THE AIRPLANE.

YOU'RE IN CAHOOTS WITH THAT THIEF.

NO WAY A KID COOKED UP THIS SCHEME.

AGH!

UH-
OH...

THE DEAL'S
OFF! IF YOU
HURT HER,
BELIEVE ME,
YOU'LL PAY
FOR IT!

!!

UH...

FORGET
ABOUT HER!
SHOOT ME
INSTEAD!!

THROW DOWN YOUR WEAPON AND PUT YOUR HANDS IN THE AIR!!

!!

!!

...

THE WHOLE POLICE FORCE IS OUTSIDE! AND THEY WON'T BE GENTLE!

I HAVE THE DRUGS! SHOOT ME AND THEY'LL ALL GO POOF!

SO DO AS I SAY!

UH...

I SAID HANDS UP!

YOU STAY OUT OF THIS!

WAIT! I WAS STILL WORKING OUT A DEAL.

WHAT ARE YOU DOING? HANDS UP!

?

TNK

HERE, TAKE IT.

Date:

Name:

Gonzo Okochi

Deed of Transfer

Details:

The individual who has signed above here transfers ownership of the aircraft specifi

Type or model of aircraft:

Aircraft manufacturer:

Aircraft number:

Aircraft registration:

CLINK

WHERE I'M GOIN', I DON'T NEED AN AIRPLANE.

HEY! WHERE'S YOUR BACKUP?!

GET WALKING!

I ADMIRE YOUR MOXIE, GIRL.

HOW'S MR. KASUGA?!

UM...

...THAT WOUND WASN'T ENOUGH TO KILL HIM.

I'M SORRY, BUT...

!!

WHEW... I'M GLAD.

AND YOU...

RIGHT. SORRY.

VALUE YOUR LIFE.

NEVER RISK YOUR NECK LIKE THAT AGAIN.

THE AIRPLANE...

Deed of Transfer

s:

ne individual who has signed above hereby
ers ownership of the aircraft specified be

IT'S REALLY MINE...

1964

*BANNER: FOR GOOD SLEEP USE YAMADA BEDDING

WOW!

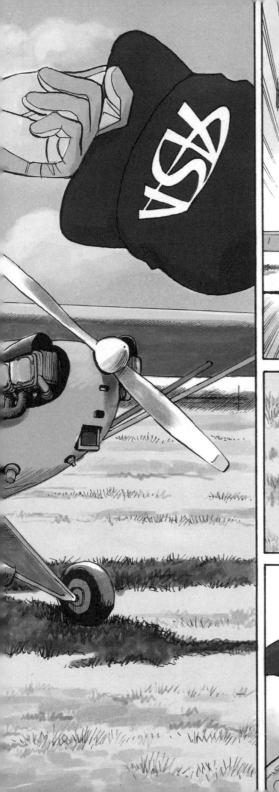

Chapter 15 ○ Age 17

THANK YOU!

THANK YOU VERY MUCH!

WHAT?! IT WAS A GIRL FLYING THE WHOLE TIME?!

LET'S HEAR IT FOR MY PARTNER TOO!

UN-BELIEVABLE! SHE'S THE PILOT!

SHE'S GOT GUTS!

Tokyo, 1964

AND WEAR A SEXY SWIMSUIT NEXT TIME!

DO IT AGAIN! ENCORE!

COME SEE US AGAIN SOMETIME!

ULP...

HUNH?!

UH-OH...

WHICH ONE OF YOU SAID THAT?!

WOULD YOU TELL A MAN TO FLY IN A LOINCLOTH?!

IT'S *COLD* UP THERE, YOU KNOW!

WAS IT *YOU*?! YOU WANNA GO UP IN A LOINCLOTH?!

N-NO, UH...

THANK YOU FOR COMING, GENTLEMEN.

SHUV

STRIP DOWN AND I'LL STRAP YOU IN!

LEMME GO! I'M FINE!

NO, YOU'RE LOSING YOUR TEMPER...

TEACH THAT GIRL PROPER CUSTOMER SERVICE!

NEXT TIME, WE'LL SHOW YOU ACROBATIC MANEUVERS AT EVEN HIGHER ALTITUDES!

BUT I CAN DO IT!

I FORBID IT. YOU'RE TOO RECKLESS.

CAN I DO A *HAMMER-HEAD?*

HEY, DID YOU SAY HIGHER ALTI-TUDES?

ABOUT THE BANNER...

MR. YAMADA! FROM YAMADA BEDDING!

STOP YAPPING AND GET THE PLANE INTO THE HANGAR.

AND FOLD THE BANNER.

URGH! WHAT-EVER!

HUH?

IT'S NOT ATTRACTING ANY BUSINESS.

GET RID OF IT.

NO...

EVEN WITHOUT IT, OUR OLYMPICS-EDITION BEDDING WILL KEEP SELLING LIKE HOTCAKES!

SIGH.

LET US KEEP ADVERTISING FOR YOU!

I'M MORE WORRIED ABOUT THE WHOLE BUSINESS FOLDING.

HUH? BUT YOU SAID FOLD IT!!

AW, JUST CRUMPLE IT UP.

LET ME GUESS...

ALL SKY AIRWAYS? HEH HEH HEH...

WHAT DOES ASA STAND FOR?

C...

IT'S BEEN A WHILE, KASUGA.

COLONEL JISSOJI! IT CERTAINLY HAS!

SKIP THE SALUTE.

THOSE DAYS ARE OVER.

RIGHT...

SO WHAT IS ASA SHORT FOR?

ASA ASADA COMPANY.

IT'S THE GIRL'S NAME.

SHE USED HER NAME IN HOPES THEY'LL SEE IT AND COME ASKING.

SHE LOST FAMILY IN THE ISEWAN TYPHOON...

...BUT SHE BELIEVES THEY'RE STILL ALIVE.

WHEN WAS HER BIRTH-DAY?

SHE'S 17. SHE GOT HER PILOT'S LICENSE THE MOMENT SHE WAS ELIGIBLE.

LOOKS YOUNG FOR A PILOT.

HOW OLD IS SHE?

...

BUT SHE CAN ALREADY FLY LIKE THAT?

UM, IT WAS YESTERDAY.

YOU TAUGHT HER WELL, AIR WARRANT OFFICER KASUGA.

SHE'S GOT SKILLS.

OOPS...

TH-THANK YOU!

Y-YES?

KASUGA...

TAKE GOOD CARE OF HER.

HUH?

WE NEED TO TALK.

...

ROAD CLOSED

18TH OLYMPICS

10/18 50 KM WALK
10/21 MARATHON

KOSHU ROAD,
SHINJUKU-CHOFU
PLEASE TAKE A
DIFFERENT ROUTE.

VAVROOM

HAVE YOU GOTTEN IN TOUCH?

THE TOKYO OLYMPICS ARE COMING UP.

THE MARATHON COURSE?

I HOPE HE'S DOING ALL RIGHT.

...BUT HE NEVER REPLIED.

I SENT A LETTER TO THE ADDRESS ON HIS NEW YEAR'S CARD...

YEAH.

WITH SHO?

WELL, IT ISN'T EASY TO REACH THAT LEVEL.

...HE'S NOT RUNNING THE MARATHON.

I CAN'T BELIEVE...

OH, HE'S "GREAT," HUH?

BUT HE TRAINED AROUND THE CLOCK! HE'S A GREAT RUNNER!

SHO ISN'T JUST ANYBODY!

NOT JUST ANYBODY CAN GO.

WELL, THE OLYMPICS ARE FULL OF GREAT RUNNERS...

...AS HE RAN THROUGH HERE.

*SIGN: PHARMACY

I WANTED TO WAVE A FLAG...

...AND CHEER FOR HIM...

LIKE WHAT?

I TOLD YOU BEFORE.

HM?

WE GOT BIGGER PROB- LEMS.

THE COMPANY IS IN TROUBLE.

YOU COULD EVEN LOSE THE AIRPLANE.

BUT WE MAY HAVE A NEW JOB.

HE'S MINORU JISSOJI, "THE KILL KING."

FROM THE MAN IN BLACK?

...I ATTENDED HIS LECTURES IN GUNNERY SCHOOL AT YOKOSUKA.

YEAH. HE WASN'T MY DIRECT COMMANDING OFFICER, BUT...

I HOPE IT'S A GOOD ONE!

AND HE'S GONNA GIVE US A JOB?!

HE'S COMING BY LATER.

...I GAVE HIM THE DINER'S ADDRESS.

I DON'T KNOW THE DETAILS, BUT...

*SIGN: SEASONAL CUISINE KINUYO

*SIGNS: (FRONT) SEASONAL CUISINE KINUYO, (OTHERS) BAR EDEN

RATTLE

WE'RE BACK!

WELCOME BACK! LOOKIN' MIGHTY PRETTY, ASA!

ASA! GET CHANGED AND LEND A HAND!

MR. LIME! IT'S TOO EARLY TO BE DRUNK!

HUH?!

SHINROKU GOT INTO ANOTHER FIGHT.

OKAAAY!

RATTLE

150円 170円 150円 150円 160円 180円

ARRRGH!

SHINROKU! HOW COULD YOU?!

IF A MAN COMES BY, SEND HIM UPSTAIRS.

YEAH! I HIT FIRST!!

BUT I DIDN'T START IT.

STOP GETTING INTO FIGHTS!

...SO KEKO GOT MAD AND SLAPPED KOSHICHI, SO I SAID IT WAS CHIKO'S FAULT, AND THEN KEKO'S BIG BROTHER CAME OUT AND WALLOPED KOSHICHI, SO I POPPED HIM ONE!

KEKO'S LITTLE SISTER CHIKO STOLE KOSHICHI'S HAT, SO I CHASED HER DOWN AND TOOK IT BACK, BUT THEN CHIKO STARTED CRYING...

HAZUKI! YOU DID?!

ANYWAY, NO MORE FIGHTING!

ENOUGH. I CAN'T KEEP UP.

AND I WAS PASSING BY, SO I SQUARED OFF AGAINST KEKO'S BIG BROTHER AND—

THAT'S RIGHT! AND I'M TELLING YOU THE SAME THING!

"WINNING A FISTFIGHT ISN'T REALLY WINNING!"

MOTHER ALWAYS SAID...

BUT WE'RE STARVING!

NO DINNER TILL YOU FINISH YOUR HOME- WORK!

YEAH, SHE'S OLD.

SIS IS A LOT LIKE HOW MOM WAS.

...17.

I'M ONLY...

TMP
TMP
TMP

HMF!

HURRY IT UP, ASA!

COMING!

TMP
TMP
TMP

WHOA, HE'S SCARY...

I CAN'T BELIEVE...

IT'S LIKE A MIRACLE.

YEAH. EVERYONE ELSE *BOUGHT* IT.

...WE SURVIVED THE WAR AND ARE ABLE TO SIT HERE TODAY.

I SPENT THE BATTLE OF MIDWAY LAID UP DUE TO PNEUMONIA...

...BUT YOU SURVIVED ON *SKILL.*

MIRA-CLE?

NOT IN *YOUR* CASE.

NAH...

LUCK?

YOUR SKILL MADE THAT LUCK.

IT WAS JUST LUCK.

IT WASN'T SKILL.

WHO IS THAT MAN?

OKAY.

ASA, TAKE THIS UPSTAIRS.

HMM...

HE WAS MR. KASUGA'S FLIGHT INSTRUCTOR OR SOME-THING.

...

THIS IS WHAT I WANTED TO DISCUSS.

I HAVE A FEELING...

...HE BRINGS BAD LUCK.

CREAM

A FISHERMAN IN SAGAMI BAY TOOK THIS PHOTOGRAPH.

*SIGN: TOKYO METROPOLITAN YODOBASHI HIGH SCHOOL

*SIGN: LIBRARY

Chapter 16 ● Don't Turn Around

WA HA HAAA! ♪ YEAH, YEAH, YEAH! ♪

DON'T TURN AROUUUND! TEE HEE HEE! ♪

IS THAT TRUE, ASA?

RIGHT, ASA?

ONLY RAISE ONE HAND ON "PLEASE"!

OTHERWISE IT LOOKS LIKE YOU'RE *PRAYING.*

HUH?

HRMM ...

YOU HAVE TO WATCH THE GESTURES! YOU KNOW THEM BETTER THAN ANYONE!

JUST CLEAN, WOULD YOU?

HRMM ...

*BOOK: EXPANDED ANIMAL ENCYCLOPEDIA, SHOGAKUKAN

増補版 生物図鑑

DO WE HAVE A BIO TEST COMING UP?

HEY!

WHAT'RE YOU PORING OVER?!

YEAH! COME ON!

WELL, STOP IT AND JOIN US!

NO, BUT...

...I'M LOOKING SOMETHING UP.

SORRY. I'M BUSY.

...BUT WE COULD BE A TRIO!

RIGHT NOW, WE JUST COPY *THE PEANUTS*...

IF ASA JOINS US, WE'LL HIT IT BIG!

UH-HUH!

LIKE MIE NAKAO, YUKARI ITO AND MARI SONO!

NO!

LIKE KASHI-MASHI MUSUME?

I'M TALKING ABOUT A GROUP.

NO, THEY'RE ALL SOLO SINGERS.

186

Chapter 16 ● Don't Turn Around

HEY...

THAT'S...

I...I'VE SEEN THAT!

ASA! GET OUT OF HERE!

OH?

I SEE IT EVERY NIGHT IN MY DREAMS!

THE DAY AFTER THE TYPHOON!

AND TOOK AWAY MY FAMILY!

IT STOMPED ON MY HOUSE!

ASA!

GO TEND THE DINER!

MMFF!!

MMFF!!

MMF!! MMF!!

THIS IS A GROWN-UP CONVERSATION! STAY OUT OF IT!

GASP!

IT'S N-NOTHING! I'M COMING!

IS EVERY-THING ALL RIGHT?

WHAT'S UP, SIS?

...

...AND FILL YOU IN LATER.

I'LL TALK TO HIM...

NOW GET GOING!

STAY DOWN-STAIRS AND TELL KINUYO NO MORE FOOD.

TUNK

LATER...

...

...THEY LEFT AND DIDN'T COME BACK.

UM...

WHAT IS IT, YONE?

HM?

WHAT ABOUT FILLING ME IN?!

HEY, WHERE'S MIYAKO?

THAT'S WEIRD. YOU TWO USUALLY GO TOGETHER!

THE GIRLS' ROOM.

UM, ASA?

MIYAKO WORKS PRETTY HARD, HUH?

WHAT'S WRONG, YONE?

SIIIGH.

YES?

YEAH, ABOUT THAT...

YEAH! BUT IT'S A HARD INDUSTRY TO BREAK INTO, SO—

...POP STARS MORE THAN ANY-THING.

HM?

SHE WANTS FOR US TO BECOME...

HM? DID SOME-THING HAPPEN?

OH, NEVER MIND.

I'M FINE. IT'S NOTHING.

YONE!

YEAH.

IF YOU DON'T WANT TO DO IT ANYMORE, YOU SHOULD TELL MIYAKO.

KIND OF LIKE A DINOSAUR.

UM, A GIANT CREATURE.

THE ZOOLOGY BOOKS HERE ARE NO HELP AT ALL.

OH, HEY. YOUR PARENTS ARE TEACHERS. MAYBE THEY CAN HELP ME OUT.

WHAT ARE YOU LOOKING FOR?

OH? IN UENO, HUH?

IT HAS EVERY- THING.

...TO THE SCIENCE MUSEUM IN UENO.

WELL, MY PARENTS ONCE TOOK ME...

I MET A SCOUT.

HEY, ASA?

HM?

FROM AN ENTER- TAINMENT AGENCY.

A SCOUT?

REALLY
?!

N-NOT
SO
LOUD!

...!!

MIYAKO
AND I
WENT TO
A MOVIE
IN GINZA
AND—

WHERE
DID IT
HAPPEN?!

THAT'S
WONDERFUL,
YONE!

WHEN
YOU'RE
WITH HER,
YOU
ATTRACT
ATTENTION!

I
KNEW
IT!

NO,
UM...

IT'S
FINALLY
HAPPENED!

I KNEW YOU
TWO WOULD
GET LUCKY!

HUH?

I CAME OUT OF THE RESTROOM FIRST, AND...

WHAT? NOT INTERESTED?

HUH? AN ENTERTAINMENT AGENCY?

*POSTER: GAZE UPON LOVE AND DEATH

OH!

B-BUT I, UM...

THEN CALL THIS NUMBER.

*CARD: MIZUGUCHI

BUT...

N-NO, IT'S NOT THAT...

THANKS FOR WAITING, YONE!

...AND SHE'D LIKE THIS TOO, SO...

UM, THAT GIRL IS MY FRIEND...

WHO WAS THAT GUY?

?

THE MOVIE'S STARTING! LET'S GO!

OH, UH... HE WAS NOBODY.

...

YOU DIDN'T INTRODUCE MIYAKO?

...

...IN ME.

...HE WAS ONLY INTERESTED...

WELL, HE SAID...

198

SHE WANTED ADVICE...

TUMP

TUMP

TUMP

TUMP

AERIAL MANEUVERS ARE *MUCH* EASIER.

TUMP

...BUT WHAT COULD I SAY?

I COULDN'T!

N-NO, UH...

"ASA, WILL YOU TELL MIYAKO FOR ME?!"

KYAH!

MAYBE I'LL FIND A CLUE HERE AT THE SCIENCE MUSEUM.

WHY DID MR. KASUGA'S TEACHER...

BUT THE CREATURE I SAW WAS MUCH BIGGER...

THAT GUY... AND THE GUY WHO SCOUTED YONE...

I DON'T TRUST ANY OF THEM!

...HAVE THAT PHOTOGRAPH?

I SHOULD BE WARY OF STRANGE MEN.

A PHOTO-GRAPH?

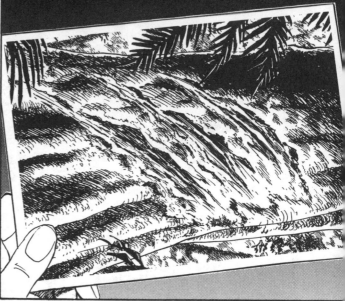

HM? WHAT'S THIS?

MMM?

!!

EX-CUSE ME, MISS.

SCRATCHES IN A TREE?

WHAT IS THIS?

204

STRIDE STRIDE STRIDE STRIDE

N-NO! WAIT, MISS!

ULP! A STRANGE MAN!

WHY DID I COME SO CLOSE TO CLOSING TIME?!

NO MATTER WHAT, DON'T DO IT!

STRIDE STRIDE STRIDE

DON'T TURN AROUND!

TAK

...WAIT!

PLEASE...

TAK

!!

WHOOOPS!!

ARGH! WHY DIDN'T YOU STOP?! I HAD MY HANDS FULL WITH THESE DOCUMENTS!

GIVE BACK THAT PHOTO-GRAPH!

IT'S VERY IMPORTANT!

Asadora! vol. 2/End

ASADORA!

To be continued...

Production Staff:
Hideaki Urano
Tohru Sakata

Cooperation:
Satoshi Akatsuka (TAC Photography)
Jun Takahashi
Nagoya Times, Archives Committee
Japan Aeronautic Association, Aviation Library
Hidetaka Shiba
Hajime Matsubara (The University Museum, The University of Tokyo)
National Museum of Nature and Science
Takeshi Ijichi (Ikaros Publications, Ltd.)
Chihiro Katsu
Nobuyuki Kojima
Satomi Danno

Editor:
Haruka Ikegawa

References:
Takahashi, Jun. *Jun-san no Ozora Jinsei, Oreryu* (Jun's Life in the Skies, My Way).
Assisted by Masahiro Kaneda. Ikaros Publications, Ltd.

Thank you to everyone else who offered help.

PAGE 173: Yokosuka, Japan, is known for the naval base United States Fleet Activities Yokosuka. The base is the United States' largest overseas naval installation. Situated south of Tokyo at the entrance to Tokyo Bay, the base is considered to be one of the United States' most strategically important military bases.

PAGE 186: The Peanuts were a vocal duo consisting of twin sisters Emi and Yumi Ito. The pair was discovered at a nightclub while they were still in high school. They went on to record original songs in the *kayokyoku* genre, a Japanese style of music that served as the foundation for modern J-pop.

PAGE 186: Mie Nakao, Yukari Ito and Mari Sono were popular singers during the fifties, sixties and seventies. The three singers starred in the teen movie *Hai, Hai Sannin Musume* (Yes, Yes, the Three Daughters).

PAGE 195: The science museum that Yone's parents took her to is the National Museum of Nature and Science in Ueno Park, Tokyo. Founded in 1877, the museum is one of the oldest in Japan and features comprehensive exhibitions of natural history and the history of science and technology.

Translation Notes

PAGE 117: The fairy tale Asa refers to is "Taro the Dragon Boy," which was originally published by children's author Miyoko Matsutani in 1960. The tale spawned several adaptations—a televised puppet series in Japan (1966), an anime (late 1970s) and an animated film (1979).

PAGE 165: The hammerhead turn, or stall turn, is an aerobatic maneuver in which the pilot flies the plane straight up until the airspeed drops to a certain critical point. Before the upward motion stops, the pilot uses the rudder to yaw the plane through a 180-degree cartwheel until the nose points straight down. The pilot then returns to level flight at the same altitude they started at, exiting the maneuver in the opposite direction.

PAGE 168: The Isewan Typhoon, also known as Typhoon Vera, was a real-life tropical cyclone that hit Japan in 1959. Isewan is estimated to have caused more than 5,000 fatalities, making it the deadliest typhoon to ever strike Japan. The widespread devastation it caused led the Japanese government to make significant improvements to its disaster management and relief systems.

Sound Effects Glossary

The sound effects in this edition of *Asadora!* have been preserved in their original Japanese format. To avoid additional lettering cluttering up the panels, a list of the sound effects is provided here. Each sound effect is listed by page and panel number; for example, "6.3" would mean the effect appears in panel 3 of page 6.

3.3 - fwap fwap (basasa: wings flapping)	**124.5** - woosh (da: running)
19.1 - vrrr (buun: airplane)	**125.1** - hwoosh (byu: running faster)
35.3 - gwooosh (goooo: fast movement)	**126.3** - screech (kiii: truck stopping)
36.1 - smash smash (baki bakli: destroying)	**128.2** - honk honk honk (paa pappaa papaa:
36.3 - hwomp (doon: footstep)	truck horns)
41.6 - bdunk (zaa: landing)	**128.4** - honk (papaa: truck horn)
45.1 - thrum vwsh (dorun dododo: propeller starting)	**133.1** - whsh (za: approaching hospital)
45.8 - vrrr (dodododo: airplane)	**133.2** - bam (dan: opening door)
46.2 - vrr (buun: airplane)	**133.3** - waaah (waaaan: commotion)
51.8 - fwsh (ba: falling)	**136.2-5** - clomp clomp clomp clomp clomp clomp
54.3 - vwoooo (vuuuuun: plummeting)	clomp (za za za za za za za: footsteps)
57.1-2 - gwooo (gooooo: airplane flying)	**151.2** - fwoosh (da: running)
58.1 - ping pang (gan kiin: bullets striking)	**152.1** - fwup (ba: entering room)
58.2-3 - brakka brakka (dodododo: gunfire)	**157.2-3** - vrrrrr (vuuuuun: airplane)
58.4 - kthunk (gashan: releasing torpedo)	**157.4** - vrr vrr (vuo vuo: airplane)
58.7 - gwoosh (goo: flying)	**158.2** - whsh (ba: flying fast)
59.8 - batatoom (dododo: anti-aircraft fire)	**158.3** - vroosh (vuon: flying)
59.8 - boom baboom (bon dodon: explosions)	**159.3** - vwoosh (vuan: flying)
59.8 - bablam (papan: gunfire)	**160.1** - swoosh (zaa: banner)
60-61.1 - ratta tatta (totatatata: gunfire)	**161.1** - pachi pachi pachi pachi pachi: applause)
60-61.1 - babababablam (papapapapa: gunfire)	**162.1** - clap clap clap clap clap clap (pachi pachi
60-61.1 - brakka brakka (dodododo: gunfire)	pachi pachi pachi pachi: applause)
62.1 - spak spakk (gan gagan: bullets striking)	**162.2** - clap clap clap clap clap clap clap clap clap
62.3 - spash (bakin: window breaking)	(pachi pachi pachi pachi pachi pachi pachi
62.3 - zing (kiin: bullet flying)	pachi pachi: applause)
62.3 - shatter (barin: glass breaking)	**162.3** - clap clap clap clap clap clap clap clap clap
62.2/4 - spak (gan: bullet striking)	clap clap (pachi pachi pachi pachi pachi pachi
65.1 - gwup (ga: gripping)	pachi pachi pachi pachi pachi: applause)
79.1 - thwap (bashii: slapping)	**163.1** - clap clap clap clap clap clap clap (pachi pachi
80.3 - hwup (da: leaping away)	pachi pachi pachi pachi pachi: applause)
80.4 - woosh (da: running)	**163.1** - clap clap clap clap clap (pachi pachi pachi
93.3 - tump tump tump (ta ta ta: footsteps)	pachi pachi: applause)
97.2 - tromp tromp (dota dota: running)	**163.2** - clap clap clap clap clap (pachi pachi pachi
97.7 - vwoosh (vuun: airplane passing)	pachi pachi: applause)
98.1 - vroosh (vuuuuun: airplane passing)	**163.2** - clap clap clap (pachi pachi pachi: applause)
98.2 - bam (don: knocking aside)	**164.3** - gwuf (ga: grabbing)
101.4 - vwoom (vuan: airplane rising)	**175.6** - fomp bomp (dota dota: stomping)
108.1 - kchunk (ga: moving lever)	**190.1** - fwap (ga: covering mouth)
108.2 - ktokk (ga: opening throttle)	**190.2** - hwoosh (ba: fast movement)
108.3 - kwunk (ga: stepping on pedal)	**192.5** - bamp (ban: closing book)
120.2 - bwunk (da: landing)	**205.6** - tumble scatter tumble (dosa dosa dosa:
121.3 - yaaay (waaa: shouting)	dropping documents)

ASADORA!

Volume 2

VIZ Signature Edition

By Naoki URASAWA/N WOOD STUDIO

Translation & Adaptation John Werry
Touch-up Art & Lettering Steve Dutro
Design Jimmy Presler
Editor Karla Clark

ASADORA!
by Naoki URASAWA/N WOOD STUDIO
© 2019 Naoki URASAWA/N WOOD STUDIO
All rights reserved.
Original Japanese edition published by SHOGAKUKAN.
English translation rights in the United States of America, Canada,
the United Kingdom, Ireland, Australia and New Zealand arranged with SHOGAKUKAN.

Original Cover Design: Isao YOSHIMURA + Bay Bridge Studios

The stories, characters and incidents mentioned in this publication are entirely fictional.

Printed in Canada

Published by VIZ Media, LLC
P.O. Box 77010
San Francisco, CA 94107

10 9 8 7 6 5 4 3 2 1
First printing, April 2021

PARENTAL ADVISORY
ASADORA! is rated T+ for Older Teen and is recommended for ages 16 and up. This series includes disaster imagery and realistic depictions of violence.

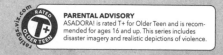

VIZ MEDIA   VIZ SIGNATURE
viz.com   vizsignature.com

This is the last page.

Asadora! has been printed in the original Japanese format
to preserve the orientation of the artwork.